First Day of School with Ji-Young

Nicole Gabor

Lerner Publications ◆ Minneapolis

Discover six early milestones alongside your favorite *Sesame Street* friends! From visiting the dentist to getting a library card, this series helps young children feel prepared for new and exciting experiences that are a part of growing up.

Sincerely,
The Editors at Sesame Workshop

Table of Contents

Starting School

On your first day of school, you might have some big feelings. You might feel excited and even a little nervous. Knowing what to expect can help.

I'm ready for my first day of school!

First Day of School

Before the first day of school, try to get a good night's sleep. You might even pick out your clothes the night before.

I'm going to wear
my checkered shirt
to school!

Grandma Nell makes me oatmeal with fruit before school.

When you wake up in the morning, it's important to brush your teeth and eat a healthy breakfast. You can also check your backpack to make sure you have everything you need.

There are lots of ways to get to school. Some kids ride in a school bus or a car. Some kids walk or ride their bikes. How will you get to school?

I walk to school in the morning.

When you get to school, you'll find your classroom. Then you'll put away your jacket and backpack and sit in your seat.

My backpack goes in a cubby that has my name on it.

Elmo learned to raise Elmo's hand when Elmo has a question.

You'll meet your teacher and classmates too. You'll learn about the classroom rules and all the fun things you'll do together.

It's fun to make new friends! Introduce yourself to the kids in your class. Smile and tell them what your name is.

Hi, my name is Abby! What's your name?

Learn to count numbers with me. 1, 2, 3!

During the school day, you'll learn lots of new things. You might practice your ABCs, learn how to count, sing songs, or do art projects.

When the school day ends, you'll say goodbye to your teacher and classmates. You'll pack your backpack and get ready to go home!

Draw a Picture of Your First Day

What happened on your first day of school? Draw a picture and share it with your grown-up. Here are some ideas of what to draw:

1. Yourself
2. Your new teacher
3. Your classmates
4. Your classroom
5. Your school
6. Your school's playground

Glossary

backpack: a bag to carry all the things you need for school

excited: how you feel when you are happy and your body has lots of energy

nervous: how you feel when you are unsure about something

teacher: a person who helps students learn

Read More

Geister-Jones, Sophie. *Back to School*. Lake Elmo, MN: Focus Readers, 2021.

Lindeen, Mary. *A New School*. Chicago: Norwood House, 2022.

Sanderson, Whitney. *First Ride on a School Bus with Tamir*. Minneapolis: Lerner Publications, 2026.

Photo Acknowledgments

Image credits: Jose Luis Pelaez/Getty Images, pp. 3, 6; dusanpetkovic/Getty Images, p. 4; skynesher/Getty Images, p. 9; FamVeld/Shutterstock/Getty Images, p. 10 (top left); kali9/Getty Images, pp. 10 (top right), 21; Images By Tang Ming Tung/Getty Images, p. 10 (bottom); FatCamera/Getty Images, pp. 12, 16; SDI Productions/Getty Images, p. 15; monkeybusinessimages/Getty Images, p. 19. Design element: Agunar/Shutterstock.

Cover: FamVeld/Shutterstock.

Index

Lerner Publications Company
An imprint of Lerner Publishing Group, Inc.
241 First Avenue North
Minneapolis, MN 55401 USA

For reading levels and more information, look up this title at www.lernerbooks.com.

Main body text set in MIkado.
Typeface provided by HvD Fonts.

Editor: Annie Zheng **Designer:** Mary Ross
Lerner team: Martha Kranes

Library of Congress Cataloging-in-Publication Data

Names: Gabor, Nicole, author.
Title: First day of school with Ji-Young / Nicole Gabor.
Description: Minneapolis, MN : Lerner Publications, [2026] | Series: Sesame Street firsts | Includes bibliographical references and index. | Audience: Ages 4–8 | Audience: Grades K–1 | Summary: "The first day of school is exciting, but it can also be scary. Knowing what to expect can help! Learn more about the first day of school with Ji-Young and her Sesame Street friends!"— Provided by publisher.
Identifiers: LCCN 2024038577 (print) | LCCN 2024038578 (ebook) | ISBN 9798765661048 (library binding) | ISBN 9798765684825 (paperback) | ISBN 9798765680896 (epub)
Subjects: LCSH: First day of school—Juvenile literature.
Classification: LCC LB1556 .G33 2026 (print) | LCC LB1556 (ebook) | DDC 371—dc23/eng/20241010

LC record available at https://lccn.loc.gov/2024038577
LC ebook record available at https://lccn.loc.gov/2024038578

Manufactured in the United States of America
1-1011809-53659-1/3/2025